Mindset Mentoring Edition

Thoughts
of A Man

A book of knowledge

YATA MCELRATH

I write for the same reason I breathe; because if I didn't, I would die.

-Isaac Asimov

Your thoughts and actions are yours. Make them count and not only be disciplined for them but be rewarded because of them.

-Yata McElrath

Mindset Mentoring Edition

Thoughts
of A Man

A book of knowledge

YATA MCELRATH

Balanced Life Publishing
Inspired to be an Inspiration

Introduction

In life, we all are seeking better, whether in our spiritual, mental, physical or financial lives. We all want better. As I have sought after, accomplished and is still seeking better. My journey has been filled with insight, knowledge and wisdom along the way by those who have taken the time out to mentor and share their life knowledge with me. Better has come in many ways, ways such as graduating college, being hired by great companies such as, Nielsen Media Research, Talla-Tron Electronics and Comcast Cable to name a few. Marrying the Queen that was designed for me, my wife. Experiencing the birth of an angel, our daughter. Writing and publishing several books. Creating Balanced *Life* Publishing and speaking to inspire and encourage many who are on that same path of being better. Being better has been and will always be a part of my life because I am seeking better so that I can inspire, motivate and encourage others to become better. Thoughts of A Man is filled with unfiltered, unselfish knowledge and wisdom that has assisted and guided me on my journey and is shared with those who will accept it as a gift to help with their journey in life.

Thoughts of A Man is a tool that will inspire, encourage and motivate you to experience the excellence that lies inside of you, if you are willing to allow it to do just that. Yata McElrath has shared this wisdom unselfishly because this same wisdom has allowed him to live better in all areas of his life and he's sharing it, in hopes that it shifts the lives of others in a way that creates better in all areas of their lives as well.

"Knowledge feeds the soul to enhance spiritual, mental, physical and financial growth."

-Yata McElrath

Be inspired, motivated, and encouraged

Thoughts of A Man A book of knowledge is an extraordinary book filled with straight to the point knowledge that is sure to inspire, motivate, and encourage you if you allow it to. Accept and apply this knowledge and don't forget to share it.

"I'm honored to inspire, encourage and motivate men to be the great men they were created to be. Man must take his mind to a place of mental, spiritual, mental and financial growth. Man and his thoughts are huge factors in creating or destroying his life. It's up to the man to take control of his thoughts to ensure his life and the lives that surround him are excellent in every area of life."
-Yata McElrath

"Every man is where he is by the law of his being; the thoughts which he has built into his character have brought him there, and in the arrangement of his life there is no element of chance, but all is the result of a law which cannot err."

-James Allen, As a Man Thinketh

"The world as we have created it, is a process of our thinking. It cannot be changed without changing our thinking."

-Albert Einstein

About the author

Yata McElrath, the man, husband, father, entrepreneur, writer, published author and speaker began writing in 2001, a past member of the Boys and Girls Club of Alexander City, Alabama Springhill division. He was awarded the first Boys and Girls Club of Alexander City Alumni of the year award. He went on to graduate from ITT Technical Institute of Technology, in Birmingham, Alabama, where he received an Associate of Applied Science Degree in Electronics Engineering.

In 2001, Yata realized he could touch and inspire people with his words and began writing with passion. He quickly came to the conclusion that everyone has a story to tell inside of them. They just have to educate themselves on getting it from their mind, to paper and then to others. He pursued his love for writing by researching his newly found love and has been writing ever since.

Yata has received writing awards for his

efforts and passion for writing. Starting with The Editor's Choice Award for Outstanding Achievement in Poetry Presented by poetry.com and the International Library of Poetry. He has poetry published in a poetry compilation called, A Surrender to the Moon.

Yata has written several books and his first book, Boys now MEN LATER inspired by, I Corinthians 13:11, when I was a child, I talked like a child, I thought like a child, I reasoned like a child. When I became a man, I put childish ways behind me. Boys now MEN LATER was written to inspire young men through their journey of life to manhood. He uses the book Boys now MEN LATER as a tool to mentor and promote growth to all boys that he comes in contact with.

His second book, Women are Gifts A Woman's Worth Vol. 1, was written to respect, repair, rejuvenate and reimburse all women for their endless dedication and commitment to life, for being women and is the gift they deserve and desire.

Women are Gifts is just the first of four from this inspirational group of books written to encourage and inspire women of all ages.

His third book, a book dedicated to his daughter, called Affirmed!, was written to affirm and awaken the excellence that resides inside of her. He made this inspirational book available to all children to be a tool that will encourage and motivate them now so that later does not destroy them.

His fourth book, the second edition to the A Woman's Worth collection called, Pleasure Principles A Woman's Worth Vol. 2 is a remarkable love story that was written to celebrate the precious gift called woman, to place a much needed light on the relationship of man and woman and also magnify the excellence of commitment.

His fifth book called, Balancing Your Life Life is like a maze but balance makes since of it. Balancing Your Life is a way of making sure your life and all of its aspects have a fair share of being and or becoming successful. Balancing Your Life will motivate, encourage and inspire you to visualize, pursue and capture your visions and dreams to assist them in becoming your reality.

Yata believes his words are gifts that must be unwrapped by all people because he writes with all people in mind. His words are truly encouraging and inspirational to all that are willing to be inspired and encouraged. He is truly inspired to be an inspiration and hopes to encourage all people one word, page and book at a time.

Yata is inspired to be an inspiration because he once was inspired. He was inspired to pursue his desires and dreams. In return, he hopes to inspire others to do the same because an inspired life will reach out and inspire another life which leads to many inspired lives.

Table of Contents

Thoughts of A Man

A man's thoughts are his first move. Before he rises from bed in the morning, before he goes out of the door to start his day and before he acts or speaks, he has to think it first. A man must arrive to a point where he can persuade his every thought that there are consequences to all of his actions whether good or bad.

As men we are made imperfect and imprisoned for our smallest of thoughts. Also, our thoughts can and will make us great men, fathers, husbands, presidents, mayors or other great leaders. If we only harvest and submit to them.

Thoughts of A Man, is a thoughtful key and is guidance for an exceptional life. It will successfully impact your life on many levels if you are willing to embrace its heart felt words.

Letter to you

You have chosen to take a journey that is required by all, a journey of thoughts, thinking and action. Thoughts of A Man will challenge your thoughts, make you think and require you to take action to obtain that which you deserve and desire.

Thoughts of A Man, was written for you and with you in mind. To encourage, motivate and inspire you to obtain and maintain the excellence in all areas of your life. You have taken the first step which is to obtain a copy of Thoughts of A Man. The rest is up to you. Use Thoughts of A Man as a tool that will assist you if you are willing to accept it.

Good luck on your journey.

CHAPTER 1 You are the answer

You are the answer to all of your questions. Even when you ask your higher power for anything you still have to do the work required for it to come to pass. This chapter will encourage and inspire you to go out with the strength that is within you to obtain all that you ask for, deserve or desire. You are the answer so go forth and gain all that this world has to offer.

A man's life

There comes a time in every man's life when he must accept his call, stand and take notice of his present state to ensure his future state. He must begin to plant his thoughts, water them with knowledge and harvest them with wisdom to prepare his inner man, husband, father, brother and friend. His harvest is designed to feed, encourage, inspire, motivate and love those that surround him whether near or far, related or not. His presence alone after his harvest will be enough to pick those up when they have fallen. His words will place many in a place of peace and sovereignty. His love will be sufficient enough to bless the masses. His favor will call unto God to unlock his dreams and desires.

He who is man is a statue of hope, a horizon of gladness and a breath of fresh likeliness. When he recognizes his harvest of thoughts are as diamonds in the ruff ready to be harvested for the world to experience his worth he becomes man. Become man, be man and place your feet on the ground that your thoughts have prepared for you to walk on. You were born to be man and for that alone places a responsibility of leadership. You must lead that which you have been given dominion over, whether it's nature, life, family or your thoughts. There is no way out of being responsible for that which has been given to you. You must own it, accept it and make it prosper because you are man. You can make negativity and positivity prosper but it's up to you to choose which one that is beneficial to a life of abundance in all areas of life. You must take the lead, be the example and at all costs make success from it.

The lost but not forgotten dad

Hey dad! Where are you? I'm looking but can't find you! You are home but, where are you? You love me but I can't feel it. You say, that you love me, but do you really? Hey dad! Where are you? I'm looking but can't find you! You were there, when I first came into this world. You said that I was your world but when you left you divided my world. Hey dad! Where are you? I'm looking but can't find you! You say that you are a man. How can you say that, when you do not even want to be a dad. A man has to be a man first, before he can even think of being a dad. Hey dad! Where are you? I'm looking but can't find you.

A dad

Through the eyes of a friend

Many don't even know how to Love a Dad. Many haven't even experienced a Dad and many don't even know how to feel sad for a Dad. Thank God for the Dad who was here during your good and bad times. My eyes as a friend saw a Dad; my eyes as a friend see your dad in you. If I can see your Dad through you, Thank God for your Dad not leaving but he now resides in you. Your Dad has left this earth but has and will not leave you. This world is here for your Dad to just pass through, So Thank God, that your Dad came, stopped and helped create you. He didn't pass through without leaving some good memories and history. I am also thankful that I was able to take part in that history which is now and will forever be His-Story. I've seen him; I saw him and will always see him in you and your story.

Race war

Realize that one race is not superior to the other. All races are similar in all areas of life. All races of people believe in something, even if, it's considered as nothing among others. All races have people with white bones, black hair, red blood, green money, thieves, killers, sinners, happy people, evil people, people that want to work, people that do not want to work, racist, big and little, small and tall, dumb & smart, disabled and able, athletic and not so athletic, selfish and unselfish, healthy and unhealthy, givers and receivers, billionaires, millionaires and poor people, people that live in big and small homes, senior citizens, babies, men, women, boys, girls, gays, lesbian, go to college & do not go to college, as you see, we are all the same one way or another which means that if you are in one of the groups does not mean that you are better it simply means there is someone out there just like you just of a different color. So ask yourself again, how are the races different? Here are a few things that segregate, separate and make us different: us, we, you, them, me, I, ourselves, this world, and statistics. Those are just a few things that makes us different and those are the things that can bring us closer together. We will ultimately win the war on race by being a great race of people.

Now and then

Stop wishing for what you know now, that you could have known it then, and use what you know now. Knowing what you know now will not help you in the past only in the future. Stop living in the past for your futures sake.

A friend

My friend

A friend loves through trials and tribulations. I love my friend, because he has my dedication. A friend must be held up without worry of cost. I hold my friend up when he needs it the most. A friend needs to be loved regardless of his situation. I love my friend without hesitation. A friend will grow through life. My friend will grow through life with me in his life. A friend is someone who is supposed to be loved to the end. I say to this world, I love my friend before and after the end. A friend must be a friend to have a friend. My friend is a friend. That is why I call him my friend. A friend is someone who is personally well known and liked. My friend is personally well known and liked by me. A friend, my friend A friend will call when he needs a friend. My friend can call because he is my friend.

A friend will talk to a friend when he has no one else. My friend can talk to me even if he needs someone else. A friend is love, is loved and is loving. My friend is love, is loved and is loving. A friend can never be alone if the love is true. My friend will never be alone because my love for him is true. A friend is family. My friend is my family.

Be different

If you are not different, then who are you? If you will not be different, then who will you be? If you are not going to be different, then you are going to be someone else. Be your own man so that you can and will own who you are.

My life without me

My life without me could never be. But is, because, God intended for me to be. My life without me. Would deprive this world of what God intended for it to see. My life without me. Would be one less life that this world could imitate. My life without me. Would be one less life that this world could appreciate. My life without me. Would be tragic if this world could not see, what God has placed in me and revealed through me. My life would not be anything without me and I would not be anything without my life. Thank you God for placing me in my life and my life in me. My life without me could never be but is, because God intended for me to be.

Men it's time to move

Men, it's time to take a stand and follow Gods plan. God has a plan for every man. We need to stop and listen. So that we can understand. To understand we must know that God leads with one hand and guides with the other. He may lead you one way or guide you to a brother. Men, I'm a brother, you are a brother. God loves it when we gather with one or another. Men, together we will stand and divided, we will fall. Following Gods plan will bless us all. When we move and stand tall. Men, it is time to listen, move, and bless when we are called. Men it's time to move.

Captured thoughts

We must take every thought captive to the point where we can persuade our every thought that there are consequences to all of our actions.

My life

My life has not always been bright. There were many days that have been blue. My life has consisted of seeing my mom beaten and seeing her lose her life after struggling to save it. As a child, my mom had less, that made my life, less. We were homeless but as I grew, that did not make my life hopeless. My life has been without a dad. This did not make me hate or become sad. I have seen my brother stay and I have seen him leave. I have seen him as a brother and I have seen him as another. I have seen friends come and I have seen friends go.

My life has consisted of miseducation and education. My life is enabling the education while disabling the miseducation. My life has been impregnated with salvation. My life is heading towards lack of hesitation and procrastination. My life was designed this way to make me a better person and man. My life is heading towards prosperity in my spiritual, mental, physical and financial life, which will cause my life to become balanced. My life will be great and my life is being shaped for this world to see and want to imitate.

Knowledge

Knowledge feeds the soul to enhance spiritual, mental, physical and financial growth.

Excellence

Excellence must consume a person before it can be produced by a person.

Are we men or not?

We are here for a purpose. To care for and love one or another. If you are a man, you must love too. If you are a man do not let love pass you. When you love, this world will be loved. It takes one to love someone for someone to be loved. Love is what should be and what is. So men open your hearts and let love in. So that this world can feel, when your love spills. If you are a boy, you are not a man. If you do not take care of your responsibilities whether good or bad.

If you run when things get bad. You are not a man. Please understand a boy is a boy and a man is a man.

His-story

(May or May not)

Be Black, World or American but it is His-Story. Deal with slaves or masters but it is His-Story. Talk about sex, money, or the degrading of women but it is His-Story. Encourage slang, Ebonics or profanity but it is, His-Story. Be politically correct or incorrect but it is His-Story. Be understood by blacks, or whites but it is His-Story. Be popular among the masses but it is His-Story. Be great in the eyes of people but it is His-Story. Be studied in any schools or colleges but it is His-Story. Will not die because it is and will always be His-Story.

Seeking perfection

I am not perfect and you are not perfect. We will never become perfect in this lifetime but there is nothing wrong with us striving for it. We may not obtain it but who knows, if we try we just might get closer than we think.

Our faith

It is said that faith the size of a mustard seed will move mountains. How will we ever experience it, if we never try to move a mountain? We must try to move the mountain first before we judge ourselves on if it can be moved or not. "Try and fail instead of failing before you try." Mountains come in all shapes and sizes; mountains can be lack of self-confidence, fear of failure, diseases, fear of meeting new people and fear of speaking in front of crowds etc. As you can see, a mountain can be anything. Having faith in something and not pursing it is worthless faith. Faith alone does not produce. Faith with works produces. -James 2:24 "You block your dream when you allow your fear to grow bigger than your faith." -Mary Manin Morrissey

Get outside of the black box

Black people we will never get to a place where we need to be if we do not remove ourselves from the black box. The black box is a place where we stick ourselves when we do not know, do not want to know or understand the way certain things are supposed to be.

We cannot move forward when we think the only way that we can advance is to act white. If acting white means getting good grades, then act white. If acting white means wearing clothes that actually fit, then act white. If acting white means taking care of your family, then act white. If acting white means speaking so that others can understand you, then act white. If acting white means respecting women, then act white. If acting white means being on time, then act white. If acting white means going to college, then act white. If acting white means paying your bills on time, then act white.

Many of us want to change or get out of our present situations but we do not want to change ourselves. When we get tired of something, we have to change or we have to change the situation. The acting white phrase is a copout for the person saying it or thinking it. That person saying it does not have the guts to change or they just do not know how to change. Therefore; they do not want you or your situation to change. If acting white means taking care of all your responsibilities whether good or bad then I will continue to act white.

If black people want to be taken seriously get outside the black box and stop looking at everything as a color or race and make your color win the race. If we as black people cannot set an excellent standard of living. Thanks white people for creating a great standard of living.

To dream is to live

Dreaming is what helps the mind to create. Dreaming makes the mind create. Dreaming is when the mind is in its creative state.

Live your life, so that your life can live. Your life can not live by itself; it also needs you to give it a helping hand.

The enemy

The enemy is not the white, the rich or the racist man. The enemy is really the inside man. We are our biggest enemy whether we believe it or not.

Springhill

Without your past your future can not and will not exist. People may not see. That Springhill is in me. They may look at my outside and ask. How can that be? You would have to walk in my shoes to see. That Springhill is in me. With doubt, again they ask. How can that be? I say take a walk with me and you will see. That Springhill is in me. They look at me in disbelief and say I have lied. In addition, I say, I to know about the other side. Again they ask, where did you lay your head to sleep? I answered by saying, I lived on Thomas Street. Since I know about the other side and Thomas Street. You should know by now that Springhill is in me. After that, you still may look and not see. However, I am here to tell you. Springhill will always be in me.

Same hood

I am from the same hood you are from. Done some of the same things you have done. Seen a lot of right and wrong. I am from the same hood you are from. I have done some things that I regret. I thank God for forgiving me for all I have done. I am from the same hood you are from. I can look passed all the things I have done. Can you? I am from the same hood you are from. Just because you are from the hood does not mean you are dumb. I am from the same hood you are from.

A few good men
The next best thing to being wise oneself is to live
in a circle of those who are. -C S Lewis

There have been many men that have
impacted my life in many ways whether they know
it or not. It's said, it takes a village to raise a child. I
used my village to help the great man rise up inside
of me. Everyone can learn something from all
people. You have to filter out what is needed for
you and your life. Make a list of great men who
have impacted you and your life to reflect and be
grateful for the wisdom that surrounds you.

Fathers

These are words from a young man who saw a father at a friend's home and not at his own home, from a young man who not only wanted a father but also needed a father and from a young man whose heavenly father placed great father figures in his life to help guide his life.

Future- a child will have a better one with the help from a father.

Attention- a child needs it from his or her father.

Time- a child needs time more than money, clothes, shoes and other material things that are of little or no importance.

Happiness- a child is happy, happier and happiest when he or she has a father in their life.

Effective- an effective father develops an effective child.

Responsibility- "A man must be responsible for all that he wants, create or desire." -Yata McElrath

Sacred- the relationship between a father and his

child or children is and must be sacred.

Your way or God's way

Don't get upset when things are not going your way. Your way may not be the right way but ask God to guide you his way. Our way prolongs and perpetuates. God's way provides, positions, prepares and promises. Don't be so quick to praise God when you are on your way but stop and ask if those things are on God's way. If God sees you going his way, he will stop and give you a ride or directions but if you are not going God's way you will find yourself on an unending road to nowhere.

You and your life are great

Who are you comparing your life to, to determine where your life should be? We are different for a reason, therefore; why should we base our existence on someone else's life? Your life is not his, hers or theirs, it's your life, isn't it? We will never be the next Michael Jordan, Oprah, Beyoncé, Bill Gates and Michael Jackson. We made those people great, now let's make ourselves great.

What others think

If what others say about you; worries you afterwards. Whose life are you living, theirs or yours? Live the life you desire so that your life will be desired by you!

I want to be successful!
Success is a favorable result.

If you don't recognize the success in your life now; you will never be successful. If you woke up this morning; your life is successful! If you have kids; giving birth is successful. If you have a roof over your head; your shelter is successful. Many are homeless. If you are employed; your income is successful. Many are unemployed. If you are happily married, your marriage is successful. Many are divorced. Successful results are spiritual, mental, physical and financial. Recognize the success in all areas of your life, so that you can be conscious of your successful life. Acknowledge the successes in your life now so that your life can be successful later. Success is a mindset and not a set of things. If you don't understand what's being said; then you are not successful.

The new slavery
Free yourself!

"The Willie Lynch Theory" strengthen the slave's body but weaken the slave's mind."

We are the master and the slave! We weaken our own spirit, mind and body and look to others to strengthen us" We weaken our spirits by not seeking God first. We weaken our minds by not reading and seeking knowledge and wisdom. We weaken our bodies by not exercising or eating healthy. We weaken ourselves by not dreaming or supporting others dreams. We weaken ourselves by hating more than we love. We weaken ourselves by accepting the easy way out. We weaken ourselves by wanting it all now, instead of building our faith and patience. We weaken ourselves by settling for second best instead of waiting for the best. We weaken ourselves by not accepting the God given gifts inside of us. We shackle our own feet with laziness and self-pity. We tie the rope, hang the rope and place our own necks inside. The race we referred to is every race and not just the black race. Slavery can be spiritual, mental, physical and financial so everyone is included. Free yourself and don't wait on others to do it for you. You have the power to do for yourself!

Let there be and there was

Let there be is a gift that we all have been given. We can use it in a positive or negative way. We have the power to let there be anything that which we want or desire.

In order to believe in the be, we must first learn to develop, condition and persuade our minds to except the fact that we have that power. Our minds must be at a place to accept that we want or desire to create.

In addition, the be is Spiritual, Mental, Physical and Financial. The be is money, health, knowledge, wisdom, power, sickness, hate, jealousy, anger, debt, divorce, ignorance, rich, poor etc. Whatever the be may be, remember that we have the power to create it. Also, our mind is the gateway to the be that we want or desire to create. Our mind has the power to open and let the be out or stay closed and keep the be in. Therefore, we must strengthen our minds in the form of education so that our minds make it a habit to let there be. Once the education settles, our mind will acknowledge the be and our bodies will have no choice but to move towards the be. Seek education and knowledge so that you can truly experience the life that you want or create it to be.

God bless America, no!

We are already blessed. If we are alive, we are blessed! If we ate today, we are blessed! If we have family, we are blessed! If we are healthy, we are blessed! If we have friends, we are blessed! If you get the point, you are blessed! So, if you are blessed, it's time to bless God. America needs to bless God for a change.

The black family

The black family is dying fast, It needs to be resuscitated; its vital signs are weak. It's being air lifted to the trauma center, it's been put on life support and its vital signs are getting weaker. The Dr. has said, "The Black Family does not have long to live because of the neglect that it has experienced over the years." People are gathering around the bed praying for The Black Family, to have a healthy recovery. The Dr. is asking them to leave because The Black Family needs to get some rest. It has experienced enough and needs time to heal. Some time has passed and The Black Family seems to be getting better. The Dr. says that The Black Family can go home in a few days. The Black Family is heading home and must go through some rehabilitation and it must go through an extensive lifestyle change to get back to its full potential. The Black Family has been referred to a therapist named

President Obama, who is under strict orders from God to not cut the black family any slack. Therapist President Obama is doing all that he can to help The Black Family but the black family is not following orders and the advice being given by its Therapist, President Obama.

Prescription for The Black Family: Fathers must pray with their family three times a day. Take Prayer before breakfast, before dinner and before bed with family. Love God, wife and kids daily without hesitation. Consult God for refills to maintain The Black Family Excellence. The Black Family must also exercise its Spiritual, Mental, Physical and Financial Body daily to maintain a healthy lifestyle.

Why chase?

Why chase things that do not want to be caught or will not enhance our growth? We are chasing jobs that are running further and further away each day. We chase jobs when our dreams are right in front of us. We are chasing money, when money must chase us. Money is the result of a product or service being bought or sold. We are not a product but we can serve. Men chase women, when the right woman wants to be caught. We chase mansions, when the apartment is not being taken care of. We chase Bentley's with bicycle mentality. We chase wealth with a poverty mentality. We chase neighborhoods, but can't leave the hood to love our neighbors. We chase the NBA and NFL, but can't catch the GPA or SAT. We chase the fabulous life, but can't catch our everyday life. We chase celebrities, but can't catch our kids. We chase TV shows that we have to pay for and are dumbing us down, but can't catch a book that is free and will build us up. We chase the future that may lie to us, but can't catch today that will be true to us. We chase love from others but can't catch the love inside of ourselves. We chase what others think of us, but can't catch our own self-esteem. We chase the good life, but can't catch the idea, that our life is already good because our God is good.

Stop chasing and believe what God already has for us, it is better than anything that we can or will catch ourselves. God supplies our needs; blesses us with gifts inside of us, which will make room for us.

It

It becomes easy when there is understanding of it. It is what you want or desire. It is spiritual, mental, physical and financial. Seek understanding of it, to control it, so that it does not control you.

Remove you from yourself

Before we can get to our full potential, we have to get ourselves out of the way. In addition, realize that much of what we do is not even for or about us. If we do not remove ourselves, we are holding others and ourselves up. When you remove self then you can get yours. We hold ourselves up more than anyone else can.

Man up!

Love your wife! Man up! Love and take care of your children! Man up! Trust and have faith in God! Man up! Go to work and provide! Man up! Fix the relationship and don't get a new relationship! Man up! Stop doing stupid and dumb stuff! Man up! Celebrate woman! Man up! Encourage a young boy! Man up! Do what's right! Man up! Stop looking for a hand out! Man up!

Our earth

Our earth is a place that is extraordinary and where we must give extra in order not to be ordinary. Our earth is great only when we come together and except our greatness. As individuals and as a group. Our earth is a place which was created for us that must be maintained by us. Our earth is a gift to us, which must be unwrapped by us to appreciate its worth. Our earth is a place which needs to be given love, attention and respect. Our earth is our shelter, our resource, our friend and can even be our enemy.

Our earth is must be treated like our dearest and present loved one so that we can pass it on to our future loved one.

Know yourself

Have you introduced you to yourself and spent some quality time with yourself lately? Are you scared of what you are really going to think or find out about yourself and just put it off until you find out by someone else? Get to know yourself now before others can tell you about yourself later. Don't let anyone know you better than you.

Prayer for my brothers

A man is made when he can master himself, pride, temptation, family and surroundings. When those are mastered, he then becomes man. It's not easy but it's not impossible. My prayer as man, God protect me from myself so that I can get to the place that I need to be that will execute your will. My prayer for my brothers, God protect us from ourselves so that we can get to the place that we need to be, a place that will execute your will.

Generational curses

We have to put an end to generational curses: divorce, high school dropout, ignorance, teen pregnancy, foolishness and unhealthiness whether they are spiritual, mental, physical or financial. We have to start now by being spouses to our spouse; fathers and mothers to our children by educating ourselves more on something that will grow us instead of kill us. Create a legacy that feed generations after you us.

Men of no color

Men of no color bring destruction to one another. Men of no color thinks less of himself and especially others. Men of no color can be white or black but that does not mean he is not a brother.

Men of no color come in many shapes and sizes but we have to treat them as brothers and most importantly love them as well as others.

Brother's keeper

Brothers you are, Brother I am. Brothers stick together when all else fails. A brother gives for and a Brother forgives. Brothers are part of Gods will. Brothers follow and Brothers lead. If it's Gods will, Brothers will succeed. If it is not Gods will to succeed. Whatever is Gods will, Brothers be pleased. Brothers you are, Brother I am. I am a Brother to you. You are Brothers to me. We can please God by being Brothers for the entire world to see.

Balanced growth
Spiritual, mental, physical and financial

Our Spiritual life holds our purpose. Our Mental life controls our purpose. Our Physical life reveals our purpose. Our Financial life is a result of our purpose.

Our Spirit holds the true meaning and the existence of our purpose. Our Mind must listen to our Spirit and realize that it controls whether we acknowledge or ignore our purpose.

Our Body reveals our purpose to us and the world, when it is in harmony with our mind. Our body cannot proceed to take action, if our mind does not tell our body to move.

Our Finances cannot reach its potential without action from our bodies, a strong mind that hungers for knowledge and a sense of urgency to listen, respect and honor our spirit.

Our purpose, happiness, money, families, dreams, wants, needs and relationships all have a place in our lives. We must be willing to understand the four aspects in our life and be mindful that they must work together to obtain all that is wanted and desired.

Obtain, retain and maintain

Will my name be in God's book at the end of my life? On the other hand, will I be escorted away from God? We must ask those two questions while walking through this journey of life.

If God has given us another day to live, let this day be the day that we answer yes to the question, 'Will my name be in God's book? God gives us an opportunity to say yes to him or to say yes to the dark side. I myself have said yes to God by accepting him into my life and believing in him to guide every aspect of my life.

To obtain a place in God's book, we must treat every day as our last because we do not know when God will return. It is best to be prepared when he comes. To be prepared means to accept God into our lives, believe with our hearts and confess with our mouths that God gave us his only son to die for our sins. We must ask God to forgive us for all of our sins (repent) and we must believe in him that he will guide all things in our lives. We must also keep God and his word in our hearts at all times.

The words obtain, retain and maintain are important in becoming part of God's book because God is keeping tabs on all things that we do. The things that we do are going to keep us in God's grace or they will push us away from God. These three words are going to help us become a part of God's book and keep us in God's grace. These three words are very important, so if you do not remember anything else remember obtain, retain and maintain.

Obtain means to acquire or gain possession of. We must gain possession of God's word. Obtaining God's word honors him. God wants us to obtain his word. To obtain God's word is to read Gods word.

Retain means to hold in one's possession, to remember. God wants us to retain the word for our lives. To retain God's word is to study God's word to the point where we remember it. Studying God's word helps us to remember it better. Think of studying the word like a high school diploma. Remember what we had to do in school to get our diploma. Think of a diploma and retaining God's word the same way. We all want to receive our diploma at the end of our lives, so we must retain God's word so that we can graduate and move to the next level, which is in God's kingdom.

Maintain means to carry on or to keep in existence. This is the best word out of the three because when you think about the definition of maintain you cannot help but like it. When we maintain God's word we glorify and magnify his Holy Name. We maintain many things throughout our lives. We maintain our marriages, homes, cars, and our bodies just to name a few and no one rewards us for doing so. God rewards us with great blessings. To maintain God's word is to pass it on to others, keep it active in our lives, which mean live by it at all times.

In conclusion, obtaining, retaining, along

with maintaining God's word are not the only things we must do to guarantee a position in God's book. The number one thing we must do is to become saved along with obtain, retain, and maintain. Those three words are not going to mean anything without Salvation but salvation also needs the aide of those three words. We must obtain salvation by accepting God into our lives. We must retain our salvation by studying God's word so that we will remember the way God wants us to live our lives. We must maintain our salvation because we need to be prepared when God comes. God will pass over the unbelievers and stretch his hands out to the faithful believers.

Remember, when we use these three words obtain, retain, and maintain with God's word and most important, with the greatest gift of all, which is salvation, a space in God's book and kingdom will be ours and well done will be the words said to us by our Heavenly Father.

Definition of the word man

Two definitions of man stand out in my mind. The first is "A man is an adult human." Simply stated, it does not mean a baby, child, or teen. All of these are humans who have not become adults. The key word in this definition is adult, which is one of the things that we have to become to help us define ourselves as men.

When I was a child, I talked like a child; I thought like a child, I reasoned like a child. When I became a man, I put childish ways behind me. -1 Corinthians 13:11

In simple terms, we cannot become men living in childish situations with a childish mind. The second definition of man is, "A male human endowed with qualities, such as strength, considered characteristic of manhood." As men, we need to strive for spiritual, physical, mental and financial strength, which are all essential for our journey to manhood.

Spiritual strength - As men we need to seek God daily by studying the word of God and in prayer to help satisfy our spiritual strength. Read, study and become a doer of the word.

Physical strength - As men we need to stay strong and healthy to help meet our needs because the good Lord needs able bodies to spread the word. Ask yourself this: what good am I to God if I have an unhealthy body? Think of your body as a car and ask yourself this question: Would I want my car to break down before it gets me to my destination? Would you want your body to break down before God gets you to your destination? Good health is very important since we know that we cannot be 100% when we are sick or hurt.

Mental strength - This is the age of information and technology. There should not be any excuses for not building a strong mind. We need strong minds. We also need wisdom with the knowledge because wisdom is the ability to make good use of knowledge.

Financial strength - Financial strength is equally important, especially in today's society. Just as our Spiritual, Mental and Physical strengths need to be up to par and so does our financial strength. We must take into account that finances in today's society can take a dangerous toll on our spiritual, mental and physical strengths. If you are not sure you believe this, think about the time when you were without money or your finances were not stable. Be honest with yourself. How did you feel? Did you think about your spiritual, mental and physical strengths? Financial strength is bigger than we may think. We need money to help take care of our life's financial responsibilities. As you can see, physical strength by itself does not define a man; it needs help from spiritual, mental and financial strength to be effective.

In conclusion, as men we must maintain our growth and consistently grow in our spiritual, mental, physical and financial lives. We need to obtain all of these strengths in order to become a well-balanced man and to understand the true definition of the word man. "By wisdom a house is built, and through knowledge its rooms are filled with rare and beautiful treasures. A wise man has great power, and a man of knowledge increases strength." -Proverbs 24:3-5

Boys becoming men

This section is directed towards older men, our fathers, grandfathers, uncles, and brothers, whom we all have or have had in our lives. These men should be or should have been a big part of the road our young boys have taken and are going to take. Older men who have seen and done more than our young boys have to take the responsibility of teaching them. Many of our older men may back down from that responsibility by saying it is not our job, but when we think about it, we must realize that it is our job.

For example, many older men have sons, nephews, and younger friends, and their jobs are to start with those people first. We can all say, "If I had somebody older in my life to sit me down and coach me, I would have traveled down many fewer roads to get to where I am today." I am not saying that older men should pull the younger men by their ears and make them listen. I am simply saying we must teach and lead by example. By doing so, we can teach them one step at a time.

Only be careful, and watch yourselves closely so that you do not forget the things your eyes have seen or let them slip from your heart as long as you live. Teach them to your children and to their children after them. -Deuteronomy 4:9

Teaching our young men to take the right roads will be a blessing to God "our teacher", the people teaching "us", and the people being taught boys and young men".

In conclusion, if we would stop being selfish and take time to teach, guide, and care for our boys and young men, we shall be blessed, and in the midst of it all we honor God by doing these deeds. Brothers, we need to start teaching our boys and young men the way God wants us to teach them. However, before we can start teaching them we must first start living our lives the way God intended.

Our surroundings

We must all understand how important our surroundings are in our everyday life. Our surroundings will make us cry and they will make us laugh they will make us good or they will make us bad.

Surroundings will vary throughout our lifetime; our surroundings may come to us as traffic jams, babies beginning to walk, sunny or rainy days. Whatever may come our way; if we listen to God our surroundings will become positive and will help us grow. The way we adapt to our surroundings is an indication of the way God works. God takes us through things that sometimes all it takes is to stop look and listen before reacting. An example is my day, which starts out by praying, eating breakfast, and praying with my wife before I get started to work. On this particular day, I did not want to go to work, but I started out anyway. I started the car and began looking at the work that I had for that day. I looked up and saw a mother walking her baby to daycare. As they were walking, I thought the baby was going to fall as she walked towards a pine cone. Instead, although her little footsteps were shaky, she managed to kick the pine cone out of the way just in time.

After seeing that baby girl walking, started a new day for me. I thought she was going to fall, just as I thought my day was going to be bad to start with. As she kicked her obstacle out of the way, I kicked my obstacle of not wanting to go to work out of the way.

By observing the little girl I stopped thinking about not wanting to go to work and took the surroundings that God put me in and used them to change my thoughts about not wanting to go to work. The reason I shared that story is that God reveals things through our surroundings that only we will see. For instance, take the story of Moses and the Burning Bush. The Burning Bush was the surroundings God put Moses in to get his attention so that he could speak to Moses. There are answers in our surroundings whether we know it or not. Exodus 15:22-25- tells when Moses was without water, God showed him a stick of wood and Moses threw it into the bitter water of Marah and the water became sweet. Moses called on God and God used Moses' surroundings to conquer the situation.

Surroundings will also make us cry. I am not going to spend too much time talking on this subject but simply to say that surroundings that make us cry are all tests, tests to show us where we are with God. For instance, we all have been stuck in traffic jams in our lifetime. Ask yourself this. How would I react if someone cut in front of me when I was making a turn? Would I curse at them, honk my horn, or would I bless them in Jesus' name? Let me help you out with the answer. If you curse at them, who is it helping, your flesh or God? Of course, your flesh. God would not curse at anyone. If you are honking your horn, whom is it helping? Of course not God, because by the time you honk, they are probably gone and you may never see them again. So, why get angry if you are never going to see them again? On the other hand, when you bless them in Jesus' name for doing the same thing, whom are you honoring? You got it! The answer is God. Let me add something else to that answer. You are also keeping a peaceful mind. A peaceful mind is one of God's gifts. Maintain a peaceful mind and not a hungry flesh, because a peaceful mind can be satisfied but a hungry flesh will never be satisfied.

In conclusion, our surroundings will always test our faith because when we ask God to guide us through our days, he will test us by putting us through things that will make us trust or doubt him and his powers. Trusting and believing in God and his powers can only strengthen us to become better people and better servants of our God. God knows what to show us. Thus we can see better and understand what he is showing us, just as he showed Moses at the burning bush.

Leading men

Men that are in leadership must come to terms and reality when dealing with or teaching our younger generations. We must not only teach, preach or just talk. The younger generation needs substance. We need to be the examples that we expect them to be. We are natural leaders so let's stop leveraging people for our own selfish gains or goals.

Lose to win
1995 Alabama 4A State Champions

While experiencing a winning high school boys' basketball record. With a goal of winning the 1995 Class 4A championship. The Central Coosa Boys Basketball Team suffered their first loss to a team who was not in any way supposed to win this game in 1995. The game was close to the end. As the clock began to wind down five...four...the shot is taken by B.B. Comer's high school point guard. Three... the ball bounces off the rim. Two... the ball bounces off the top of the backboard. In any other game this would have been a turn over or out of bounds. But in this case, one...the ball bounces off the backboard and into the rim. Buzzer sounds. Game is over. Central Coosa has just been defeated by B.B. Comer. Coach Belyeu is pleading his case to the referees to have that play overturned but to his dismay the team had started celebrating and the game was officially over.

The Central Coosa Team walks off the court in total shock, confusion and anger. As they sit in the locker room and wait for Coach Belyeu to come in and address the team. They could only guess or imagine the effects that it took on him being that he was also living a dream of winning his first championship. Coach Belyeu comes in like normal but completely shocks the team with these words. "You lost this game for a reason. You needed to lose this game. You needed to lose this game to know what it feels like to lose. Now that you know what it feels like to lose. You can get it out of your system and win the rest of your games." Those words alone were life changing and profound at that moment and in this moment. Once you go through something, you now know what it feels like. Now you can get it out of your system and win the championships in your life. Central Coosa boy's high school basketball team went on to win the first championship in Coosa County history with a record of 31-1. Thirty-one wins and one lose.

Family unit

When the family is strong it is everything and anything that you need. Lose a mother, father, brother, sister, aunt, uncle or even a friend and a family will give you another. Family is the strongest corporation or organization ever created and should be treated as such.

Purpose filled life

Your purpose is the gift given to you to help you live a meaningful and abundant life. Your purpose was created when you were created. It was embedded inside of you at birth. Your purpose is a part of you just like every part of your entire body. It's no different than any of your organs that help you live. Your purpose is an organ. It's the organ that supplies meaning to your life. It's the part of your life that helps your life live.

Your purpose doesn't care about your past. It doesn't care about how poor you are, if you were abused, if you lived in the projects, if you had a child at an early age, if you dropped out of school, if you made bad decisions or even if you came from a single parent household. Your purpose only cares about now.

Your purpose hungers to be fed. You are the only one that can feed that hunger in order to operate in your purpose. Nelson Mandela was a man that operated with purpose. He may have passed away but his purpose will be remembered forever. When you operate in your purpose, your purpose keeps you living even after your body passes away. What will you be remembered for and will it be worthy of living forever? Your purpose can not be denied. It's yours and only you can realize it. You were designed specifically for your purpose and it is your duty to manifest it.

As you were conceived your purpose was also conceived. As you grew and took form in your mother's womb, your purpose was also growing and taking form. As you were born and began to take on this journey called life, you began taking steps to find your place in life. Some begin to find their place sooner than others but we all have a place and purpose. We just have to listen to that which is deep inside of us. Listen to it, believe it, obey it and receive that which keeps us awake at night. That silent voice that sounds right to our spirit and heart. That thing which gets us excited even when times and circumstances say otherwise.

Our purpose calls unto us on a continuous basis. It is not selfish and has others in mind. It wants us to answer its call. It wants us to follow divine directions to be allowed and released to the world.

Your life is being robbed of success, greatness and excellence in all areas of your life when your purpose is not honored or exercised. To keep your life from being robbed of its glory, get out there and discover the purpose that awaits your arrival.

Changed mindset

Asking or telling someone to change their mindset is easier said than done. Asking or telling someone to change their mindset is like: A smoker telling another smoker to quit, an alcoholic telling another alcoholic to quit drinking, a broke person telling another broke person how to get money. It's nearly impossible to tell or ask someone to change a mindset that they have been living with all of their life. I'm guilty of telling someone to change their mindset but didn't come to an understanding that it was impossible to get them to change. The only way to get someone to change their mindset is to get them around someone that is going where they want to go or has been where they want to go. I've come to the conclusion that people don't change their mindset unless they have a reason to change. Like someone showing them better or something happening in their life that is so drastic that they have no other choice but to change.

Our dreams are alive

We have become so busy and or lazy that we have mistreated, abused and aborted our dreams due to immaturity, lack of education and selfishness.

We mistreat and abuse our dreams by procrastinating. Our dreams are calling on us to make them reality but we ignore them by not taking out the time to nurture them. By not doing, asking or seeking help and knowledge on helping our dreams grow or mature.

We abort our dreams by giving up on them too soon or giving up on them all together before they manifest or take form. We were impregnated with our individual dreams at the beginning of our conception. Just as we grew in the womb, our dreams were also growing and becoming one with us. When we were born and came into this world our dreams were incubated inside of us until we were able to come to realization that we had a dream, vision and purpose inside of us. When we become aware of our dreams, our dreams are at the place of being born. The time between conception and birth of our dreams are different for us all. Also, the times of birth of our dreams are different for us all. Many have established or recognized their dreams at early ages, mid ages, later ages or some die without giving birth or experiencing their dreams.

As I stated before, our dreams were placed in us at birth but are not realized by us until we start to yearn for our meaning of life or existence.

In 2000, I was told to ask God to reveal my purpose but if I didn't want to know, to not ask because once to question is asked. God has no choice but to reveal it to you and then it's up to us to receive it. I asked in 2001 and my purpose was revealed to me. The purpose was inspiring, encouraging and motivating others through writing. Once my purpose was revealed, my dreams became clear but not before the pains of fear and lack of courage took over. Those were the labor pains I had to endure before my dreams would be born and realized by myself and others.

Time to think

There comes a time in every man's life, when he must think. That which he chooses to think is his responsibility. Just as he chooses to think he must choose to be responsible for the outcome of his thoughts. His thoughts are what separate him from the majority. They keep him from being normal or even mediocre. His thoughts are anger, happiness, fear, lack and riches to name a few. He is his thoughts, if his thoughts are of anything. Then he becomes what he thinks.

CHAPTER 2 Notes from my Mentor

A mentor is one of life's precious jewels that many people are unaware of. There are mentors all around us. We just have to be courageous and focused enough to go out and ask for help. Find a mentor that is specific to your goals, dreams and aspirations. Mentors will encourage, inspire and motivate you to get to your place in life but you have to do the work. Go out and seek, find, retain, maintain and share the knowledge that you are so worthy of.

This chapter is comprised of real accounts of Yata McElrath's mentors sharing their thoughts and wisdom. So take this knowledge and wisdom as a gift and use it to create a better place for your life.

3/15/2012...6:30 pm

Great men are great because they first think of greatness and then they pursue that greatness with an urge to succeed or die trying attitude.

4/19/2012...5:10 pm

Keep your thoughts at bay (bay being inside your mind) until it's time to take them out to sea (sea being the world). Once out to sea, throw them over board and watch them sink or swim. The ones that swim will keep you grounded as you get back to dry land. Leave the ones that sink to drown and buried at sea. The thoughts that swim are thoughts of positivity, encouragement and motivation etc. The thoughts that sink are thoughts of negativity, fear, lack and failure etc.

7/10/2012...1:25 am

When we let entertainment trump education, we lose! Don't spend the majority of your time being entertained if you want to be great. There's a time and place for everything and entertainment can't take all of your time or be in every place. Spend your time becoming great!

10/4/2012...9:10 pm

Take control of your thoughts but don't let your thoughts take control of you. Your thoughts can be your worst enemy if you don't control them with caution.

1/11/2013...2:20 pm

Cars and clothes ownership are not near important as business ownership or home ownership. Prioritizing your life is an important key to success. Own that which will enhance all areas of your life. Success will help you afford the nicer things in life but stuff will not create success in your life.

3/17/2013...7:15 pm

A career or job doesn't give you the same quality of life as being a business owner. Careers and jobs create a great quality of life for the business owner. The business owner create the careers and jobs.

5/3/2013...8:15 pm

Those that are determined, serious and courageous to try to succeed are not responsible for the ones who are not. We are only examples and obligated to help or encourage those who are willing to go the same extra mile that it takes to reach success.

8/23/2013...5:00 am

Believe in yourself to the point that nothing or no one can change your mind about the vision that was given to you from above.

9/25/2013...7:00 am

The people you hang around are a direct reflection of you. When see your closest friends you see yourself. If they are broke, rich, wealthy, healthy, positive, determined, happy, negative, fearful, courageous, hardworking or loyal. Then you are too. If they are reaching for the stars or doing nothing. Then you are too. Take inventory of the people around you and if they are headed in the same or higher direction, then cherish those relationships but if not sever them quick.

11/12/2013...9:12 pm

We must use every moment as a time to learn. We can learn from everyone. Whether good or bad, everyone can teach you something. They can teach you what to do and what not to do. It's up to you to filter out all that you need or don't need. A rich man can teach how to be rich and poor; rich in finances but poor in family affairs. Which will you choose? A poor man can teach you how to spend; spend time with family, money and time on foolishness. Which will you choose? A man can teach you how to love and hate. Which will you choose? Learn the lessons that grow you as a person and will take you to higher levels in life.

1/25/2014...8:15 pm

Living requires present action and gains fuel as the future becomes closer. Living now creates a life in the future so don't discredit living now because your future is depending on you now.

5/1/2014...5:15 am

Suits create while uniforms make. The closer you are to wearing a suit within our marketplace is when you create more money, time, productive relationships, wealth and freedom. Successful businesses and people are run by the people in suits and those that are employees wear uniforms. Suits control many of our thoughts and actions on a daily basis by collaborating with like and smarter minded people. If you want real freedom you have to become a suit/creator.

6/15/2014...10:13 pm

When negativity consumes your spirit, mind, body and finances. Your spirit will produce hate, your mind will produce confusion and fear, your body will produce sickness and your finances will produce lack and poverty.

7/10/2014...6:30 am

Allow yourself to be open to new experiences, ideas and people. You have to get outside of the box to obtain most of what you want out of life, especially, those big dreams and ideas that cross your mind from time to time. The box is for those people who are comfortable with life and who are not willing to go further. If that's not you, then jump out of the box and run without looking back.

11/14/2014...5:00 am

A man is where he is because he chooses to be there. A man's choices are his and he is the one who must be held accountable because of them.

CHAPTER 3 Mindset Mentoring

When the mind changes; everything else changes.

Mindset Mentoring was written to challenge your mind and to encourage you to remove your box instead of getting outside a box that so many believe that they are in.

We all want better in some form or another. Whether it's spiritual, mental, physical or financial, we all want better. Mindset Mentoring is a tool that will help you conjure up the better that lives in your mind. Everything forms in the mind and our bodies are the vessels that assist those things in becoming our reality.

Unclean

It's not what goes into a person that makes them unclean, it's what comes out of them. What's coming out of you that makes your life unclean?

Giving up

There was a time when I was contemplating giving up on writing and becoming an Author. Then I realized that the time I was wasting on contemplating was the time I needed to write. Don't substitute your dreams with things that will prevent you from obtaining your dreams.

Being at peace

Those who cross or try and disrupt your path are the ones who lose because you're at peace in all areas of your life.

Marketplace or commonplace?

Marketplace is where hundreds of thousands, millions and billions are made. Marketplace is where the rich, guided, fearless and those who apply knowledge reside. To reach the marketplace, the mindset has to change. Commonplace is where cents and dollars are made. Commonplace is where the poor, miseducated, fearful and foolishness reside. To stay in a commonplace, the mindset will not change.

The vision

The vision will require some hands on from all parties who will benefit from the rewards. Nothing more pleasurable or rewarding than when your rib partakes in the vision. Love this woman more and more each day. The vision will sometimes require some form of work but will not be realized without work.

God gave

God gave us so much but we traded, sold, donated or just gave it away for ignorance, fear, lack, nonsense, foolishness, miseducation etc. Accept what God gives. Use and share it to benefit your life and others lives.

Prayer changes but only with action.

Matthew 21:22- Whatever you ask in prayer, you will receive, if you have faith. Praying for others is a must and a kind gesture but if the recipient doesn't act accordingly they lose for the time being. To pray or receive prayer requires action from both participants. To do nothing but pray and both participants lose. Pray and act accordingly! Pray for others and hope they act accordingly.

Paying it forward!

If you don't at least step away from your environment even if it's only temporary. You will continue to be a product of it. To be uprooted is a form of growth. A growing and healthy plant can't stay in the same pot all of its life. It eventually has to be repotted to grow bigger.

Live on purpose

A lack of purpose is what's keeping many in a defeated state of mind and reality. Without purpose a man will continuously feel as though the world is pressing down on him in all areas of life.

Purpose takes you to a place where nonsense, foolishness, ignorance and lack can't thrive. Those things exist and will forever exist but purpose will shelter you from the blows. Discover your purpose and live your life on purpose! Ask, believe, obey and receive your purpose because your life deserves it!

Get rich or die being poor?

Reality is perceived differently on many levels. The poor who choose to stay poor will never understand the reality of the rich but there are many of the rich that does understand the reality of the poor.

The poor must stop complaining and focus on becoming rich in ways that benefit them and stop hoping and praying that the rich will miraculously feel a need to be poor and give all of their riches away. The rich is in no way obligated to hand over anything but they do provide some ways of relief such as jobs which are stepping stones for increase. The poor is obligated to seek and learn of ways to better themselves and should not want handouts for a better way of life.

Being rich or poor are both choices. Deciding to live better is a choice. Ignorance is a choice. Settling is a choice. Riches will not flow down from the government, job, pulpit or thin air without a vision, plan or action that will sustain it.

Choose today whether you want to be rich or poor in any area of life: spiritual, mental, physical or financial. We must choose and stop being content and lazy if that's a true destination for us. There is a rich mindset and a poor/poverty mindset. How does your mindset measure up? It's one of the two. Be honest and if it's not rich, you have work to do.

Be rich in your spiritual, mental, physical and financial lives. Riches are not only financial but many have been programmed to believe and accept that fact.

In all you do get understanding

The words God reveal to you are just as or more important than what any man can say to you. A Pastor says to the congregation, "Come to church and hear what God has to say to you!" My thoughts, if church is where you go to hear from God, you are not listening very well. We are the church so if we come to ourselves and our senses we will indeed hear from God. Timely sermons are preached if you listen closely, consistently and with confidence in God. The word you need has already been shared with you.

Minimize your distraction so you too can hear from God. Your personal kingdom must be consistent before the kingdom can be effective.

You are the answer

God will give you strength. Others will give you a hand but it's you who have to do the work. You must move. You must do something. You will have to ask, believe, obey and receive. You are the answer to anything that you deserve or desire.

Pastors must build people first before buildings

Let's put the focus on building people instead of buildings. When the people are strong their environment and dealings become strong, stable and indestructible. Build up the people's hearts and minds and all other things will be blessed. Sermons are like prescriptions with the side effects causing more harm than the issue itself. The people need solutions more than a simple sermon.

Issue: People are hurting in all areas of life.

Prescription: Two hours of singing and sermons. The people are not shown how to apply the word. They are just told to take it and they will be healed.

Side Effects: Discomfort, uneasiness, restless spirit, brokenness, confusion and miseducation.

Solution: 2-3 hours of the strong people

(congregation) in a certain area rallying around those that are weak in that area.

Disclaimer: We all have to be honest, the weak and the strong. We all have to stop acting like we have it together and be willing to share our weaknesses and strengths.

Don't let tradition bind your mind

When tradition causes you to do the same thing over and over again in hopes of different results and the results are the same. You are in a place of insanity and your mind has become bound.

A new you

A new you will only experience newness. Don't participate with the status quo by just saying and following the lead of oldness. Start today with a new book, new idea, new thought, new dream, new word or a new vision and become a new you.

THOUGHTS OF A MAN

No excuses

Four pounds PREMATURE at birth didn't stop my growth. SINGLE PARENTING didn't stop the multiple blessings in my life. The PROJECTS didn't and doesn't define me. POVERTY didn't break me. DEATHS didn't stop me from living. FAILED RELATIONSHIPS didn't and doesn't affect my marriage. STUDENT LOANS didn't keep my income from growing. JOB didn't stop my business from being created. BAD BOOK DEAL didn't stop me from writing. $5.15/hour didn't discourage me from dreaming. HOMELESSNESS didn't stop me from owning a home. MISEDUCATION didn't and doesn't stop me from reading and seeking knowledge. Witnessing my Mom's physical and mental ABUSE from other's and herself didn't and doesn't stop me from loving my wife and daughter. SHYNESS as a kid didn't stop me from

A BOOK OF KNOWLEDGE   140

speaking to kids or pursuing a dream of motivational speaking. FOOD STAMPS didn't cause me to depend on the government for the rest of my life. You can stop all of your excuses because they will only distract you. Excuses are designed to set you back so why not move forward with No Excuses.

Be in control

Don't let others have more control over your purpose or destiny than you.

Seek knowledge

Knowledge feeds the soul to enhance spiritual, mental, physical and financial growth. Be educated more than entertained   Education lasts a lifetime; while entertainment lasts until the TV show or concert is over.

A good life

A good life is not a perfect life but I've found out that a great life is a well-balanced life. Balance your spiritual, mental, physical and financial lives and live a great life.

God speaks

God speaks so eloquently, if we allow ourselves to hear him by eliminating distractions.

Disappear and say nothing

Sometimes you must disappear to be seen and say nothing to be heard.

God's gift

God kept you alive and now it's up to you to unwrap the gift of life and live!

Don't limit your understanding of God

When we don't read the bible for ourselves we limit ourselves of the knowledge within ourselves and the word of God. Don't allow others interpretations or words to be your only source of understanding. Others interpretations or words may limit your growth because of their level of understanding or misunderstanding. Don't limit your growth waiting on others to tell you what the word of God says.

Purposed life

I truly believe that a lack of purpose is what's keeping many in a defeated state of mind and reality. Without purpose a man/woman will continuously feel as though the world is pressing down on them in all areas of life.

Choose heaven or hell

There is hell, earth and heaven. We are in the middle of heaven and hell. We are in between heaven and hell. We are halfway to heaven and halfway to hell, here on earth. God gave us a mind to choose heaven or hell. It's your choice.

Your story is being written

Your story wants to be realized whether you want it to be realized or not. You will have to do things that will scare you or make you uncomfortable. Your story is a part of your life and you must live it out in order for your story to be realized.

Your story is being written and you may be hindering it with fear or miseducation or by doing what's common or a part of the norm. Live your life so that your story can live and inspire, save, encourage or motivate a life.

Yourself to blame

When the mind changes; everything else changes. When everything does not change, you have yourself to blame.

Having fun

Don't have so much fun that you accomplish nothing. Entertainment is just that, entertainment! But many of us don't know when to turn it off.

Deserving dreams and desires

We can't afford for the heavens or universe to be pierced with others negative thoughts, ideas or sarcasm concerning our dreams. So we must protect our dreams and desires until manifestation. Some have our best interest at heart. Some are wishing for the demise of our dreams and don't even realize it. Many could care less until they realize our dreams. Our dreams and desires deserve to live regardless of what others think.

Becoming better

Being or becoming better is for you first before you can assist anyone else in being or becoming better. Be better in ways that your presence alone rubs off on others.

What's on your mind?

If what's on your mind not moving you forward or making you better. Release it!

Where's your loyalty?

Even if the devil lives, we don't have to give him life. When you acknowledge the devil more than God, your loyalty is proven.

Where are you going?

Doing something leads somewhere and doing nothing leads nowhere.

Who are you listening to?

If you are moving towards better, quit listening to people who are not. You will become fearful, negative, lazy, miserable and complacent and a quitter if you consistently listen to people who have a negative outlook. Speak better and greater into your own life.

Grown man

Young boy cool and fun is different from a grown man's cool and fun. Young boys enjoy the world while grown men enjoy life. The world should revolve around your life and not your life around the world.

Thinking Man

A man's thoughts are his first move. If his thoughts are going nowhere then he will go nowhere but when his thoughts are consistently progressing, then he will progress to a multitude of greatness.

Real Man

A real man takes care of all of his responsibilities whether good or bad. He knows and understands that all that he creates, deserve or desire is his responsibility and no one else's. He will hold true to his word and believe that which comes to him is because of his belief and action towards it. A real man truly understands and will not be misunderstood because his actions are real.

CHAPTER 4 Applied actions

Your life is a result of all of your thoughts and actions. Be mindful that in order to succeed. You will have to think and act a certain way. This chapter is a continuance of knowledge that if applied just as the knowledge before. You will succeed in all that you were created to succeed at.

Poverty mindset

Poverty mindset is alive but can be destroyed when the mind becomes strong. We can't wish, make or pray poverty away. We have to take action and make it go away.

Entrepreneur mantra

Never concern yourself with who will not but only with who will. We can't please everyone but we can please someone.

Who are you associated with?

If you are associated with a broke, busted, negative, lazy, irresponsible, miserable, inconsistent and ignorant person and you are not making them better, then they are making you more like them.

Make up your mind

You know what you want. Now make up your mind and go get it.

American dream or nightmare

A job and career are two stepping stones to the American dream but can also create an American nightmare. The surest way to the American dream is to own your own business, create a great product or provide a superior service.

Work your butt off

A young man who I mentor calls and after talking with him, he says, "You make things look easy! You write and speak with ease. Nothing seems hard for you and everything seems to go your way." I respond, "I'm glad you see it that way but I work my butt off."

Young people to get what you want in and out of life, you have to work consistently to maintain that life and become better at life. You will have to work your butt off.

Maximize your potential

Maximize your potential by minimizing your distractions. To extend your intentions To give birth to high expectations To place abundance in all your operations To bring forth new inventions To free action and put chains on procrastination To win the race for others to be blessed in your space To show the world the light that shines in your face To be the evidence that wins your case To show there is light in you To be what you need as you go through To kill false and give birth to true To help others not hope but believe in you To set your price and not settle for a price To be sufficient and proficient To gain access to or possess excellence To be the secret ingredient To bring forth life to end all strife To be the life that comes alive. In order to survive: Maximize, maximize, maximize!

Don't wait but create!

Why wait when you can get busy and create. If God would have waited nothing would have been created. Don't wait for a job, create a job! Don't wait for love, create love! Don't wait for happiness, create happiness! Don't wait for a way, create a way! Don't wait for time, create time! Don't wait for success, create success! Don't wait for millions, create millions! Don't wait for a leader, create a leader! Don't wait for a smile, create a smile! Don't wait to be last, create a way to be first! Don't wait for greatness, create greatness! Don't wait for a great future, create a great future! Don't wait for excellent kids, create excellent kids!

Manifesting a dream
The dream and your dream

The way that we manifest a dream is to stop being selfish. Once we remove ourselves out of the way to serve others our dreams can be realized. Many people need us to realize a dream whether it's to see our dream or us encouraging them to manifest their dream.

The way that we manifest the dream is to understand the "I Have a Dream speech" by: Dr. Martin Luther King Jr., not to get into the whole speech but think about what he did, he spoke!, he spoke things into existence, he spoke things that were not as though they were, he envisioned things past the environment that he was in. I'm simply saying there is power in what you speak. Speak sickness and you become sick. Speak ignorance and you become ignorant. Speak hate and you become hateful. Speak being poor financially and you become financially exhausted. Get it? Speak your dream regardless of your environment. Speak your dream regardless of your circumstances. Speak your dreams because your reality and future depends on it.

Who wants to be a pooraire?

Pooraires have big TV's and rims and think they are important.

Millionaires have big libraries, big ideas and big resources. Pooraires watch TV to find out what's going on.

Millionaires read books to find out what's going on.

Pooraires are grown.

Millionaires are always growing.

Pooraires make money to spend money.

Millionaires spend money to make money.

Pooraires want to be taken care of.

Millionaires take care of.

Pooraires complain.

Millionaire's campaign.

Pooraires destroy.

Millionaires create.

Pooraires are changed by their environment.

Millionaires change their environment.

Pooraires consume more than they produce.

Millionaires produce more than they consume.

Pooraires are the smartest one in their circle.

Millionaires have smart people in their circle.

Pooraires take generational curses.

Millionaires give generational blessings.

Pooraires think they are stuck.

Millionaires know they are free.

Pooraires can't see past today.

Millionaires plan for tomorrow.

Improving yourself

Don't spend more time upgrading and improving your phone, cars, and homes than you do upgrading or improving yourself.

The process

Too many try and figure out the process to be successful but fail to find out, that all that who become successful do the same thing but do it with different work. The key is to figure out your work first and then study those who are successful. You will quickly find out that they became successful because they found their work and not because they did anything special. Find your work and you will understand the process. The process is the same it's the work that's different.

Out of order

When you go to a vending machine and see that it has a sign on it that reads, "OUT OF ORDER". You don't proceed by putting money in it because you understand that you will not receive what you want. So why do you continue to support, purchase or be a part of those things that don't yield any results or growth in your life. Don't continue to expect those things in your life that are "OUT OF ORDER" to yield results in your life because they will just stand there and yield nothing.

Simple but effective!

I've been asked how to write a book? The answer is one word, sentence, paragraph and page at a time. Just as everything in life that can be accomplished. It takes one step at a time. The hardest thing to do is start but once you've started you have to continue until it's complete.

To lose ten pounds, starts with one pound. Write a book, starts with one word. Get a job, starts with one application. Saving money starts with one dollar. To be nice, starts with one kind gesture. Understanding the bible starts with one scripture. To stop smoking, starts with giving up one cigarette. Unwavering faith starts with one faithful act. Start with one thing and see it to completion to experience effectiveness in your life.

You are the answer
What, when, where, why and how

What, when, where, why and how are questions we have asked and have pondered what the answers may be. There are many answers to many questions but the answer to a great majority of our questions is you. You are the answer to your questions.

If you want anything, you have to do something to obtain it. If you want a job, you have to create a resume, apply and interview for the job. If you want a car, house or clothing, you have to obtain a job to provide all of those things. If you want to be happy, you have to create an environment for you to experience happiness. Those are a few examples of you having to do something to get something. You can't have anything worth having if you are not willing to do something to obtain what you want. You can ask for or believe in anything but you still have to do something to receive that which you deserve or desire.

Thank You

Yata McElrath and Balanced *Life* Publishing would like to thank you for your support in purchasing this book, that was written with you in mind and written for you to be inspired, motivated and encouraged to accept and experience the greater, that lies inside of you.

We hope that Thoughts of A Man A book of knowledge helped you awaken your greatness. Please continue to support Yata McElrath and Balanced *Life* Publishing for their efforts in inspiring, motivating and encouraging others.

Balanced Life Publishing, LLC

Inspired to be an Inspiration

http://balancedlifepublis.wix.com/balancedlifepublish

Thoughts of A Man

A book of knowledge

ISBN-13: 978-0979193668

ISBN-10: 0979193664

www.ingramcontent.com/pod-product-compliance
Lightning Source LLC
Chambersburg PA
CBHW060013050426
42448CB00012B/2740